Striving for Peace

Striving for Peace

The Legacy of Yitzhak Rabin

Foreword by
Rt Hon Tony Blair MP

Introduction by
David Cairns MP

LABOUR
FRIENDS
of ISRAEL

First published in Great Britain in 2005 by
Labour Friends of Israel
BM LFI
London WC1N 3XX
www.lfi.org.uk

A CIP catalogue record for this book is available from the British Library.

ISBN 0 9500536 7 8

Typeset in Minion

Contents

Acknowledgements

Labour Friends of Israel would like to thank all those who have contributed to this publication and whose insights and efforts, we hope, will further understanding in Britain of the situation in the region and help strengthen the UK's role in the peace process.

Foreword

by Rt Hon Tony Blair MP

The ten years following the death of Yitzhak Rabin have often been difficult ones in the Middle East Peace Process. But despite the difficult and sometimes tragic day-to-day developments, the foundations for peace, laid down by Rabin whilst he was Prime Minister, still exist today.

Yitzhak Rabin was instrumental in setting the parameters of the peace process, now widely accepted, that a resolution to the Israeli-Palestinian conflict would be based on a negotiated settlement, leading to a two-state solution.

All those who met Rabin, as I had the pleasure to do, could not fail to be struck by his strength of character. It took a very particular type of courage and determination to take the first steps towards peace. Although his life was tragically cut short, we can at least give thanks that he was able to exercise a position of leadership at a key time in Israel's history.

As someone who attended his funeral, I experienced at first hand the sense of mourning felt not just by Israelis, but the whole world at his loss. Rabin changed our expectation of how the Middle East could be. The fact that his funeral in Jerusalem was attended by the representatives of a number of Arab states is testament to that fact.

It is fitting that Labour Friends of Israel has chosen to commemorate the life of Yitzhak Rabin by publishing this pamphlet. He symbolises many of the values that I, and so many of my Labour colleagues, admire most about Israel – a commitment to democracy, justice, liberty and progress. Israel's ability to sustain its way of life, open government and strong democratic tradition under the most difficult circumstances is rightly respected.

What Yitzhak Rabin understood is that a negotiated agreement between the Israeli and Palestinian people is the surest way to ensure Israel's future as a stable, secure and democratic society. His advocacy of this position took both leadership and vision.

By meeting the challenges of the coming months and years with both resolve and determination, we can achieve real progress to stand as a fitting tribute to the memory of one of Israel's greatest statesmen.

Introduction:
Striving for Peace

by David Cairns MP

The impact of a great leader goes far beyond their lifetime. They have the power, not only to inspire those who come into contact with them and those who are led by them, but the following generations that learn of the sacrifices they made for their people. Yitzhak Rabin will forever be remembered among the canon of great Israeli leaders, as a statesman of the world and more than that, as a peace maker. Even when he was still alive his achievements, both as a soldier and politician, were legendary. Now that he is no longer with us, he remains an icon of the peace movement in Israel and beyond.

It was with that in mind that Labour Friends of Israel decided to mark the tenth anniversary of Rabin's death by commemorating his life and legacy with this fascinating collection of essays. The purpose is not only to celebrate the life, achievements and values of an extraordinary man, but to assess, ten years on, the impact of his life's work.

To that end, in addition to personal recollections and tributes from individuals who knew Rabin and worked with him, this collection evaluates the Oslo process, the most recent Israeli steps to peace, and the challenges of the future.

Part I of the book brings together tributes to Rabin from those who admired him from near and far. Personal accounts from those close to Rabin convey the impact he made on those around him throughout his life. His daughter Dalia, herself a former Knesset member and Deputy Defence Minister, writes of her own determination to continue the struggle for peace that her father has come to symbolise. She explains why, for the sake of Israel's legitimacy, Israel has no other choice than to pursue negotiated coexistence with her neighbours.

Senior Labor Knesset member Ephraim Sneh, a minister in Rabin's government, who regarded him as a mentor, has contributed an article he wrote one year after Rabin's death. Printed here in English for the first time, with a special update from the author, the article portrays the painful sense of loss in the aftermath of the assassination and the sense of responsibility felt by those left behind.

This collection takes particular interest in the relationship between Rabin and British political life. Eminent historian Sir Martin Gilbert, famous for his histories of Israel and of Winston Churchill, unites these themes in his revealing account of a tour he gave to Rabin of Churchill's wartime bunker in Whitehall. Though encountering very different challenges, the ability to bear the responsibility of leadership in times of war and peace, clearly connects the two Prime Ministers.

The theme of responsibility is also taken up by Leader of the House of Commons, Rt Hon Geoff Hoon MP, whose personal tribute exemplifies the respect and admiration of politicians within the British Labour Party for Rabin as an individual. He reflects also on the values that Israel shares with the UK – a commitment to democracy and the rule of law – along with the shared threat to these values posed by terrorism.

In Part II, a host of senior experts help explain Rabin's political and strategic thinking, and how he sought to balance Israel's security imperative with the need to build a lasting peace with her neighbours.

Professor Shlomo Avineri, one of the fathers of Israeli political science and head of the Israeli Ministry of Foreign Affairs during Rabin's first premiership (1974-1976), reveals that, over twenty years, Rabin was remarkably consistent in his approach to the Palestinians. He shows that Rabin never doubted the need for territorial compromise and negotiated settlement when the timing and circumstances were right.

Dr Rory Miller, of King's College, London, gives an overview of the relationship Rabin built with the UK and its leaders over the course of his political life, and how that relationship reached new heights during the period of the Oslo process.

The importance of the peace process for Israel's own democratic legitimacy is the theme of Dennis Ross's contribution. The former US envoy, a central figure in the peace process throughout the 1990s, stresses Rabin's understanding of Israel's need to share land with the Palestinians as vital for sustaining Israel's Jewish and democratic character.

Dr Colin Shindler, of the University of London's School of Oriental and African Studies, examines the climate of tension within Israeli society that preceded Rabin's murder in November 1995. He goes on to consider the impact of the assassination on the development of the peace process in the months and years that followed.

Part III of the book relates Rabin's legacy to developments ten years on. Isaac Herzog, Labor Minister for Construction and Housing in the current Israeli Government, explains the huge significance and difficulty of Israel's withdrawal from Gaza and part of the Northern West Bank, and draws the connection to Rabin's own controversial steps for peace. His enduring faith in the project started by Rabin testifies to the fact that the seed of peace, once planted, has had the strength to endure, despite the storms it has weathered in the intervening years.

Looking from outside the Government, Professor Yossi Mekelberg, a Fellow of the Royal Institute of International Affairs (Chatham House), compares the approaches of Yitzhak Rabin and Ariel Sharon towards territorial compromise and assesses what the disengagement might mean for the future of the peace process.

Finally, this collection would not be complete without remembering Rabin in his own words. Though not a politician famed for colourful oratory, his apt and honest choice of words at key moments, including at the signing of the historic Oslo Accords in Washington in 1993, are well remembered by all who heard them. Here, the speech given by Rabin on receiving the Nobel Peace Prize in December 1994 has been reprinted.

His words and message, though simple, are deeply moving. On reading them, one is overwhelmed by a sense of Rabin's great humanity and by the sense of his regret at the wars he had to fight in defence of his country. Above all, one is struck by his dedication to the notion of the 'sanctity of life', and his desire to end suffering and death on all sides. One cannot escape the conclusion that it was Rabin's experience of war that fuelled his willingness to take great risks for peace.

All politicians understand that no leader is perfect and that no-one makes the right decisions all the time. But we judge the greatness of our leaders by their determination and integrity in acting on the values they believe in. The peace process begun by Rabin was not perfect, and it has not proceeded smoothly or without cost. But the vision that Rabin was willing to embrace, of a negotiated settlement with the Palestinians and all Israel's neighbours, and the values at its core – democracy, freedom and co-existence – continue to inspire leaders in Israel and around the world.

It is not only Rabin's achievements in life but the direction he showed to those who follow him that will ensure his legacy, of striving for peace, will endure in the years to come.

David Cairns is Member of Parliament for Inverclyde and former Chair of Labour Friends of Israel.

Part I

Soldier of peace: memories of Rabin

Continuing my father's quest: Israel's only choice

by Dalia Rabin

The tenth commemoration of the assassination of my father, Prime Minster Yitzhak Rabin, it is a fitting time to reflect on his achievements and legacy.

The name of Yitzhak Rabin will forever be connected to Israel's ongoing struggle for independence and survival – beginning with the bitter battles of the country's War of Independence in 1947 and 1948. As commander of the forces which secured the road to Jerusalem, Rabin laid the cornerstone for a life devoted to the security of the State of Israel. During his service as Chief of Staff of the Israel Defence Forces (IDF), Rabin prepared the military and ultimately led the execution of its most famous victory – the 1967 Six Day War.

Leaving military life to pursue a role in shaping the country's political development, Rabin continued to serve Israel by accepting the position of Ambassador to the United States and establishing a new era of cooperative diplomacy between Israel and the US He later became a minister in the government of Prime Minister Golda

Meir, and continued to rise through the ranks of the Labor Party until reaching the pinnacle of his career, serving two non-consecutive terms as Prime Minister (1974-1977 and 1992-1995) and as Defence Minister (1984-1990 and 1992-1995).

It was during his second term as Prime Minster that Rabin undertook the challenge which would carve out a new and defining role for him in Israel's history – that of 'soldier of peace'. His vision was to create a secure, democratic and prosperous Israel, living at peace with its neighbours. To this end, he changed national priorities and invested heavily in education, national infrastructure and in Israel's periphery.

He realised that to truly be secure, democratic and prosperous, Israel would need to reach reconciliation with her Palestinian neighbours. His visionary course of action tore down many seemingly insurmountable walls as he established peace with Jordan, opened a dialogue with North African and Persian Gulf nations, undermined the Arab boycott and initiated and ratified the Oslo Peace Accords with the Palestinians. These unprecedented strides toward peace reflect the two mainstays of Rabin's life – protecting the security of Israel and ensuring its continued growth and viability through the ongoing quest for peace.

The Oslo Accords were an historic breakthrough. For the first time, Israelis and Palestinians agreed to recognise that bilateral negotiations are the only means to resolve the conflict and accepted the notion of coexistence through separation.

Two weeks before he was assassinated in 1995, Yitzhak Rabin told former US Secretary of State Henry Kissinger that Israel had entered the Oslo peace process because it had no choice. Or rather, it had three options regarding Gaza and the West Bank, but only one was a valid choice. The three choices were integration, that is, a move which would change the demographic basis of the State of Israel, creating a bi-national or non-Jewish state; an Arab 'Bantustan' solution, which would create an apartheid-like existence that would destroy the moral basis of the state; or negotiated coexistence.

Yitzhak Rabin chose negotiated coexistence. In so doing he was continuing a path that began at Camp David in 1978, when Menachem Begin became the first Israeli leader to recognise the legitimate rights of the Palestinian people, and continued at the Madrid conference in 1991, when then Israeli Prime Minister Yitzhak Shamir began a process of negotiations with Palestinians. Rabin saw the Oslo Accords as a natural continuation of the process that began at Camp David and continued at Madrid. Indeed, he insisted that the terminology used in the draft of the Oslo Accords be the same terminology used in the Camp David Accords.

Rabin's decision to choose negotiated coexistence was the motivation behind Oslo. Weakness was not behind it but might, combined with the profound understanding of its limitations. My father was not lead or mislead, not duped nor manipulated. He knew exactly what he was getting into, what the price was and what he was receiving in return. He understood the risks and shortcomings, the alternatives and the limitations.

As soon as the Oslo Accords were signed there was criticism from left and right. The Israeli right saw the accords as surrender and capitulation. The Israeli left saw them as too vague. They avoided the most difficult questions of Jerusalem, Palestinian refugees and the right of return, as well as the issue of a Palestinian state and final borders.

Rabin believed that approaching these explosive issues at such an early stage would kill the process and that, instead, it would be wise to move forward through a series of interim agreements. By progressing cautiously and carefully, enough trust would be built to allow the two sides to deal with the emotional and existential issues of Jerusalem, refugees and final borders.

Indeed, five years after my father's assassination, we saw that an attempt by then Prime Minister Ehud Barak to forge a comprehensive agreement that would embrace all of the issues – including the difficult ones noted above – at a second Camp David conference hosted by President Clinton, lead to a total breakdown of the diplomatic process and to the resumption of violence.

Had Yitzhak Rabin been allowed to carry out the process that he began, would we have witnessed the same breakdown? Would Israelis have suffered over the past five years from merciless terror? We will never know the answer to these questions. But what we do know is that since his departure, his greatest critics have now accepted his approach: Israel has no choice but separation from her Palestinian neighbours. The recently completed disengagement from Gaza and the construction of the separation fence between Israel and the West Bank is a direct continuation of this policy, albeit that the present Israeli government is taking these steps unilaterally and not as a result of negotiations.

And thus, today we see the main legacy of the Oslo process. Oslo represented a mind-shattering change of tactics between two enemies. The hesitant handshake on the White House lawn represented an acceptance that the conflict can only be resolved by compromise. Until that moment, the goal for both sides was to vanquish the enemy. From that moment on, the goal became to learn to live with the enemy side-by-side, in honour and in peace. That goal remains elusive and, at times, seemingly unapproachable. But it has been adopted by the vast majorities of both the Israeli and Palestinian electorates, and their leaders. This is perhaps the most important component of the legacy of Oslo: the realisation that one side will not emerge the victor and the other the vanquished, but rather that the destinies of both nations are mutually dependent.

It was with this knowledge that Yitzhak Rabin decided that it was time to give peace a chance and to take the risks needed to fulfil the obligation and make it a reality.

The choice is still the same and there remains only one option: negotiated coexistence. In just five years' time – in 2010 – there will be a majority of Arabs living between the Jordan River and the Mediterranean. The option of integration does not exist, unless we want to forgo the Jewish character of the state. The status quo – ruling over millions of Palestinians against their will – is not an option, unless we want to become an apartheid state. Just as this was true in 1993, the same is true today – the only choice is negotiated coexistence with our Palestinian neighbours.

Despite the immense challenges, I remain committed to my father's vision of creating a secure, democratic and prosperous Israel, living at peace with its neighbours. This is the essence of his legacy and I intend to do all within my power to bring it to fruition – the alternative is unthinkable.

Dalia Rabin is the daughter of Yitzhak Rabin. She is a former Knesset Member and Deputy Minister of Defence and is now the Chair of the Yitzhak Rabin Centre.

Return to Rabin's way

by Ephraim Sneh MK

This article was first printed in Hebrew in the Israeli newspaper Ma'ariv in 1996, on the first anniversary of Rabin's assassination.

The autumn winds and the changing of the seasons evoke memories of the days preceding the murder. The violent battles over the second Oslo agreement, the last trip to the United States, the manifestations of violence and incitement, the tension leading up to the rally in the square, the terrible night.

The longing for Yitzhak intensifies, but the growing and overwhelming feeling is that of rage. We know that the murderer succeeded, he achieved his goal. He is sitting now in his cell, smiling his arrogant, filthy smile. He wished to halt the peace process and indeed it has been halted. Even if the interim agreement will be carried out, and this is highly doubtful, it is clear that no additional agreement between us and the Palestinians, between us and any Arab state, will be signed in the next four years.

Worse than that, everything that Yitzhak Rabin built, with thoughtful effort, over the course of forty months, is being destroyed and erased. The agreements with the

Palestinians created a new coalition in the Middle East – a peace coalition, opposing Islamic extremism and terror. At its centre was the square: Israel, Jordan, Egypt and the Palestinian Authority; at its periphery the North African and Gulf states. This was the new regional order, adding to Israel's security and a firm political standing ...

... The economic achievements which were the fruits of peace, Rabin's source of pride, are being erased. Foreign investments and tourism are declining. The final chords of his action-filled life – the closing of the circle of the Six Day War victory by achieving peace with his former enemies – are fading away.

Nowadays, a different wind is blowing in our country. We are the only democratic state in which a political murder has strengthened the murderer's side, rather than the victim's. This casts a heavy shadow over our democracy.

But worst of all is the danger of war. The war which Rabin so wanted to prevent, the bloodshed, the anguish of losing friends, which Rabin wanted to spare from the young boys and girls who cheered him in the square – this desire that was the deepest motive for his actions in his final years. That desire gave him the inner strength to stand up to those who wished him dead.

The date of Rabin's death is a day of soul-searching for his followers, his comrades and for anyone who does not wish his road to come to an end, or for hope to be lost. The pain, the longing, the anger, must be translated into action, with the aim of bringing Israel back to the road of sanity and peace.

Yitzhak's eyes glance at us. Only if we do not forsake his heritage, only by continuing in his way with determination and persistence, will we be able to look straight into them.

In 2005, Ephraim Sneh writes:

I wrote these words nine years ago, on the first memorial day of Yitzhak Rabin's murder. Two things have occurred since then.

Firstly, the war that Rabin tried to prevent broke out. It was an inevitable result of the stalemate created by his assassination. Hundreds lost their lives in the war we call 'The Second Intifada'.

Secondly, Israel pulled out of Gaza. Many of those who incited against Rabin came to the conclusion that the occupation is harmful for Israel. Not one of those apologised for the harsh words they said about Rabin when he was still alive. The construction of Israeli settlements in the West Bank and Gaza has proven to be a colossal, historic mistake. Most Israelis today support dismantling some of them as a reasonable price for a two-state solution.

What has not changed in those years?

The Israeli-Palestinian conflict has not been resolved. The withdrawal from Gaza is not a substitute for such a solution. It may yet serve as a pretext for another political stalemate, followed by another round of bloodshed, if serious negotiations are not resumed.

Ten years on, Israel has not yet returned to Rabin's way. It has to, urgently.

General (ret.) Ephraim Sneh is the Chairman of the Labor faction in the Knesset. He was Minister of Health under Yitzhak Rabin and subsequently served as Deputy Minister of Defence and Minister of Transport.

Rabin in Churchill's War Rooms: remembering a Prime Minister

by Martin Gilbert

It was my good fortune to have met Yitzhak Rabin a number of times during the last twenty years of his cruelly truncated life. Our first encounter was during his first premiership, when I was drawing the maps for the second edition of my Atlas of the Arab-Israel Conflict. It was shortly after the United Nations' resolution of November 1975 equating Zionism with racism. I had drawn a map showing all the countries – among them all the Arab countries and all the Communist countries – that voted in favour of this pernicious resolution.

Rabin studied the map carefully for several minutes. I did not like the look on his face. Then he told me, with blunt frankness, that, by itself, this map would not do. It was essential, he said, to show the other side of the coin; to face the map of the anti-Israel nations with a map of those countries that had voted against the resolution. They were the 'real' countries, the great democracies, the countries with liberal and humane values.

Far from complaining about those who voted in favour of the resolution, Rabin urged that we should be proud that Israel was supported by so many decent countries, thirty-five in all, including Britain. How right he was. I did as he suggested and it is one of the most important pairs of maps in the atlas.

I learned a lesson that morning that I never forgot, a lesson that Rabin continued to teach to anyone who would listen: that Israel was a country that had no need to hang its head in shame, or to regard itself as a pariah nation.

When, in July 1992, Rabin became Prime Minister for the second time, this point was an important aspect of his first speech in the Knesset. As he told the Israeli legislators: 'No longer are we 'a people that dwells alone' and no longer is it true that 'the whole world is against us'. We must overcome the sense of isolation that has held us in its thrall for almost half a century.'

Rabin was a determined negotiator. He had held secret talks with King Hussein in London in 1985. His peace treaty with Jordan a decade later, negotiated in tandem with Shimon Peres, was a model of its kind. Land was returned to Jordan without an outcry. Rabin and King Hussein found a bond that he would never find with Yasser Arafat. It was a bond of men who had seen the harsh reality of war and were determined that their two countries would not go to war with one another again.

John Major became British Prime Minister at almost the same time that Rabin was returned to power in Israel.

Soon afterwards, Rabin came to London. He and Major were to have talks all morning, but the talks were postponed when Major had to go to Buckingham Place for an emergency discussion about the status of the Princess of Wales in the event of the Queen's death. While Diana was separated but not divorced from Prince Charles: would she or would she not become Queen?

Major had to make an announcement about this in the House of Commons that afternoon and so Rabin was left with no morning talks. I was asked to look after him until Major could return from the Palace. I took him to the underground Cabinet War Rooms, a short walk from Downing Street.

Rabin was not amused to have been asked to be a tourist. He looked distant and annoyed. In the room used by Churchill and his War Cabinet, I pointed out that on the War Cabinet table was a desk calendar opened at the climactic day of the Battle of Britain. Rabin was motionless and unimpressed. I told him that I wanted to quote the text of one of the telegrams Churchill had sent that day.

Rabin looked totally disinterested. I then began quoting Churchill's telegram. It was to the Mayor of Tel Aviv. Rabin looked vaguely interested. It was a telegram of condolence – Rabin was a little more attentive – sent by Churchill following the death of more than a hundred Jews in an Italian air raid on Tel Aviv the previous day. Rabin was suddenly transformed. His face lost ten years. From bored passivity he moved in an instant to total engagement. And then he spoke. For half an hour he held us all entranced.

Rabin had been in Tel Aviv that day. He had just finished his morning swim and was walking home along Bograshov Street. As he walked he heard a roaring sound. The Italian warplanes were over his head, flying inland along the line of the street he was on. Then they dropped their bombs, only a few hundred yards in front of him. He was one of the first to come upon the scene of carnage. As news of the bombing spread, his father had come out to search for him, afraid that he might have been one of the victims.

We continued to walk around the Cabinet War Rooms. When we came to the charts showing the U-boat sinkings in the Battle of the Atlantic, Rabin questioned me intently about the details of the sinkings, and how closely Britain had come to being starved out. He asked me to send him more details of that moment – a black one in Churchill's life – when it looked as if Britain would be brought to its knees. He was profoundly interested in the vulnerability of great nations, seeing parallels with Israel's own vulnerability.

Two years later, in the summer of 1995, I accompanied John Major on his official visit to Jerusalem, Gaza and Amman. As a result of the Oslo agreements, Arafat had returned from Tunis and taken up his chairmanship of the Palestinian Authority. Rabin asked Major to impress upon Arafat that the imminent elections in the Palestinian Authority must be free and fair. In the discussion in

Jerusalem, I was impressed by how wary Rabin was of the verbal and even written promises of Chairman Arafat.

Rabin was no man's fool. He pointed out that Arafat had refused to make the pledge to abandon violence an integral part of the Oslo agreements. Instead, he had 'relegated' it to a separate letter between the two men. This, Rabin felt, was an ominous sign, putting, as it did, the promise of an end to violence outside the formal framework of the signed agreements.

When I returned to Israel in the autumn of 1995, Rabin asked me to come and see him. He was in the Prime Minister's office, smoking his usual heavy smokes and looking worried. The topic he wished to discuss was Islamic fundamentalism. What concerned him was this: that whenever an Islamist terror act took place, people saw it as a localised, far-distant, nothing-to-do-with-them phenomenon. There was no recognition that this was a global phenomenon that affected all nations simultaneously.

Rabin spoke about a number of recent incidents, close in time but scattered geographically. He urged me to map them and to stress in an explanatory text that these apparently diverse incidents were in fact linked. I was impressed by the strength of his conviction. Today we understand all too well, or ought to, what he was saying a decade ago.

When I said goodbye to Rabin that day, he was looking forward to his next visit to Britain. He told me that one pleasure he always had – after the formal dinners and speeches of any visit was over – was to get together over a glass of beer with the Mahalniks: the men and women in Britain who had gone to Israel in 1948, as volunteers, to fight in the War of Independence, when the very existence of the new state was in danger.

These men and women, the veteran Mahalniks, were Rabin's special pride. He delighted in their company just as, almost half a century earlier, he had admired their courage.

On the day after Rabin's assassination, I had, by chance, to speak at the annual Mahal reunion in London, an event planned many months earlier. In front of me in the hall were forty or fifty elderly men and women who under Rabin's command had experienced the heat of battle. They were tough and hardy types. But as I spoke a few words to them about Rabin's life, from every part of the hall came a strange, unfamiliar, muted sound: of men and women weeping.

Sir Martin Gilbert is the author of Israel: A History. The eighth, updated edition of his Arab-Israel Conflict Atlas has just been published by Routledge.

Rabin, Israel and Labour: shared values and aspirations

by Rt Hon Geoff Hoon MP

When I last had the privilege to visit Israel, as the United Kingdom's Foreign Office Minister responsible for the Middle East, I wanted to pay my respects at the grave of Yitzhak Rabin. As I stood there looking at his gravestone, together with the hundreds of others who daily attend to pay their own respects, I was reminded of something he said in his lecture on receiving the Nobel Peace Prize in 1994. He told the story of the image he saw whilst flying over the country in an aeroplane. He said he looked down at the earth below and gazed at:

> Deep blue lakes; dark-green fields; dun-coloured deserts;
> stone-grey mountains; and the entire countryside
> peppered with whitewashed, red-roofed houses. And
> cemeteries. Graves as far as the eye can see. Hundreds of
> cemeteries in our part of the Middle East.

Not only did Rabin capture something of the country's great natural beauty, but also a sense of its tragedy. Like so many of history's great peacemakers, Rabin was, for much of his life, a man of war. He was called up to serve his country at the age of 16. It was not what he wanted. He later admitted:

> That was not my dream. I wanted to be a water engineer.
> I studied in an agricultural school and I thought that being
> a water engineer was an important profession in the
> parched Middle East. I still think so today. However, I
> was compelled to resort to the gun.

His ambition may have been to become a water engineer, but history had a greater destiny for him. He began what was to be a military career of great distinction in 1940, serving in the 'Palmach', an elite unit of the Jewish 'Haganah' defence force. He went on to command the IDF during the 1967 Six Day War as Chief of Staff.

Understanding Rabin's life as a soldier is the key to unlocking his motivation and his contribution to politics. In many ways he was the embodiment of the Israeli people during his time. He had spent so many years in the Army, fighting to defend the young and fragile State of Israel. Many have said that Rabin was a hard man. He was certainly tough – he needed to be. To use an Israeli saying, Rabin was a 'true sabra' – the fruit that is hard and prickly on the outside but tender within. He knew as well as anyone the realities of war and, perhaps because of his experience, he knew the lasting value of peace. But Rabin knew also that there can only be lasting peace through mutual security.

When Yitzhak Rabin led the Labor party to victory in the 1992 Knesset elections, he was still seen by the Israelis as a soldier. But perhaps because of this, he proved to be the ultimate pragmatist. He knew that Israel 'lives in a difficult neighbourhood'. He also knew the price the Israeli people had paid for living in a permanent state of conflict with her neighbours. If Israel was to prosper in the future, he knew that there had to be an accommodation with her Arab neighbours, but one that guaranteed Israel's right to exist in security.

The Israeli people believed that they could trust Rabin. He was the great general who had served his country with distinction and courage. Like the Israeli people, Rabin was weary of war but was always a true patriot. Many felt that he lacked the warmth and charisma of his friend and colleague Shimon Peres, but they understood that Rabin, together with Peres, was the right man to lead a negotiated settlement without compromising on the vital interests of the country. And crucially, because Rabin rightly enjoyed this tough reputation, he could perhaps go further than others.

Many said Rabin was a man of few words. Some even dubbed him blunt and aloof. Perhaps he was. But he allowed his achievements speak for themselves – the most eloquent testimony of all.

His assassination on November 4, 1995, dealt a hammer blow not only to the State of Israel. His death was a loss felt throughout the world by everyone who wanted to see peace and progress in the Middle East. His award of the Nobel Peace Prize in December 1994, together with Yasser Arafat and Shimon Peres, had given renewed hope in the Middle East. The promise of an enduring peace with the

Palestinians sadly did not proceed as he would have wished, but his legacy is one of fervent hope for what can be achieved.

Under Rabin, Israel's standing in the world reached new heights. Anyone who doubted his contribution on the international stage needed only to witness the array of world leaders who attended his funeral – from President Clinton to King Hussein of Jordan. That is why I was so privileged to be asked to help commemorate the 10th anniversary of his death through Labour Friends of Israel and to mark the memory of a man who is rightly remembered as the 'Soldier of Peace'.

Labour Friends of Israel in the United Kingdom plays a significant role inside Parliament and beyond. It is rightly one of the biggest organisations inside the Parliamentary Labour Party. The events it organises are essential to promoting a greater understanding of the State of Israel, as well as promoting support throughout the Labour Movement for the Middle East Peace Process based on a two-state solution.

The organisation has also worked to foster co-operation with the Palestinian community. Conferences, such as the 2003 gathering at Ditchley, have brought both sides together, and recent delegations, which have included Labour MPs and other opinion formers, have included visits to the Palestinian Authority in Ramallah. The work of Labour Friends of Israel ensures the British Labour Party is actively engaged in the region and helps to ensure that the United Kingdom is respected and influential in its development.

Israel and the United Kingdom share many values and aspirations but we also, sadly, in the present time, face many common threats to these values. International terrorism has been faced by the people of Israel for too long. The twisted ideology of the suicide bomber has nothing at all to do with the true teachings of Islam or the views of the vast majority of decent, hard-working and law-abiding Muslims. But those terrorists who wish to destroy our freedoms and way of life – whether on the streets of Tel Aviv or Beslan, in Washington or Madrid, in Bali or in Britain – can never be allowed to triumph. And the creation of a peaceful and just settlement in the Middle East, based on an Israel safe and secure in its borders, living in peace and harmony with a viable Palestinian state, remains a huge priority for the Prime Minister and the British Government.

On receiving the Nobel Peace Prize, Rabin spoke of the responsibility and duty we in public life shoulder. He said:

> I was a young man who has now grown fully in years. And of all the memories I have stored up in my seventy-two years, I now recall the hopes. Our peoples have chosen us to give them life. Terrible as it is to say, their lives are in our hands. Tonight, their eyes are upon us and their hearts are asking: how is the authority vested in these men and women being used? What will they decide? What kind of morning will we rise to tomorrow? A day of peace? Of war? Of laughter or of tears? A child… cannot choose his father and mother. He cannot pick his sex or colour, his religion, nationality, or homeland. Whether he is born in a manor or a manger, whether he lives under a despotic

or democratic regime, it is not his choice. From the moment he comes, close-fisted, into the world, his fate lies in the hands of his nation's leaders. It is they who will decide whether he lives in comfort or despair, in security or in fear. His fate is given to us to resolve.

Yitzhak Rabin was a man of vision. In these often difficult and sometimes dark days, all of us who strive for a lasting peace in the Middle East should take great encouragement from his memory. He was bound to his people, their struggle and their suffering because he had been part of it all his life. But he also believed in a better future for his people. His vision lives on. His life continues to inspire people the world over – a decade after that life was so tragically taken.

Rt Hon Geoff Hoon MP is Lord Privy Seal and Leader of the House of Commons. He has previously served as Secretary of State for Defence and Minister for the Middle East in the Foreign and Commonwealth Office.

Part II

Security, democracy and coexistence: Rabin's policy approach to peace

Rabin's strategy: understanding security and the limits of power

by Shlomo Avineri

When, in 1995, Prime Minister Yitzhak Rabin signed the Oslo Accords with the PLO and shook, however reluctantly, Yasser Arafat's hand on the White House lawn, a lot of commentators were surprised by what they viewed as his transformation from a hard-headed general, focused on security, to a peace-maker. The contrast however, was at least in part artificial and did less than justice to Rabin's complex and nuanced views on the Arab-Israeli conflict.

In January 1976, I was appointed by the government as Director-General of Israel's Ministry of Foreign Affairs at the recommendation of Foreign Minister Yigal Allon. Before assuming my position, I had a long talk with Rabin. He had become Prime Minister in 1974 after the government of Golda Meir, which included such veterans of Israeli politics as Abba Eban and Moshe Dayan, had to resign in the wake of the 1973 Yom Kippur War.

At our meeting, Rabin enquired about my views regarding the possibility of talks with the PLO. Several times I had voiced the opinion that under certain conditions Israel should talk to the PLO, a position which Rabin opposed. I gave the Prime Minister my assurances that so long as I served in the government, I would follow government policies. If I would feel the gap between my personal views and official policy too deep, I would resign – I always had the option of going back to my university position.

I think I satisfied Rabin on this, so I asked if I may ask him a policy question. Assuming the role of Prime Minister in the post-Yom Kippur War atmosphere of crisis, Rabin had pointedly avoided making statements about his ultimate goals regarding relations with the Arab countries and the future of the occupied territories. He led a traumatised nation, a deeply wounded Labor Party and a weak and rickety coalition. I said to him that I understood his reluctance to go out on a limb and expose himself to criticism either from the right or the left. But since I wanted to be able to follow, and defend, government policy, I needed to hear from him, for my own enlightenment, his views on the future of our relations with the Arab countries and what should be the ultimate fate of the occupied territories.

After admitting his political difficulties, Rabin launched into a lengthy analytical exposé of his strategic and political thinking. The following is based on notes I took at that time.

Ultimately, Rabin said, Israel could not and should not hold on to most of the territories it captured in the Six Day War. Specifically, it cannot hold on to the West Bank and

Gaza, since ruling 3 million Palestinians against their will is unacceptable to Israel as a democratic state and will never be countenanced, even by Israel's staunchest friends. Hence he opposed Jewish settlements in the territories, with the exception of the Jordan Valley and parts of the Golan Heights.

Eventually Israel should agree to withdraw from almost all the territories except Jerusalem, but the major issue is timing. According to him, this could not and should not be done when the country is still traumatised by its initial failure at the Yom Kippur War and the Arab countries are still intoxicated by their tremendous successes at the beginning of the war, especially the dramatic crossing of the Suez Canal. Any Israeli withdrawal at this stage would be viewed by the Arabs as proof of their military success and would be interpreted as the beginning of an overall roll-back movement, ultimately aimed at the elimination of Israel.

In order to make it possible for Israel to offer what would be ultimately extremely generous territorial concessions – almost a full withdrawal – a number of conditions would have to be fulfilled, so that Israel's concession would not be interpreted as a sign of weakness, particularly given the context of the Cold War:

- The Israeli army, badly demoralised and still licking its wounds despite its ultimate successes in the Yom Kippur War, would have to be rehabilitated.
- The Israeli public would have to be convinced that the war has not sapped the national morale.

- Likewise, the Arab countries had to be convinced that they would not be able to use outside diplomatic pressure on Israel.
- The US strategic commitment to Israel had to be deepened and turned into long-term arrangements. Only such a secure anchoring would signal to all, including the Soviet Union, that the final arrangements in the area were not to be an outcome of Israeli weakness.

Only if these conditions would be fulfilled, and for this Rabin estimated a period of 3-4 years, could Israel seriously consider negotiations about the final status of the territories. In the meantime, a series of interim agreements should be undertaken, to show that there is momentum.

Regarding the Palestinians, Rabin said he would prefer an agreement with Jordan (which after all ruled the West Bank prior to 1967). Negotiating with the PLO, he argued, would mean creating a Soviet client-state at our door step and, given Soviet attitudes to Israel, this 'would be madness'.

I was impressed then, as I am today, by the sophistication and complexity of this analysis. I also understood why, given its layered nature, it could not be explicitly stated. Yet, to use common metaphors, it combined a strategic 'dovish' long-term strategy with a tactical 'hawkish' short-term public stance. By trying to reach further interim agreements with Egypt, and by maintaining close though clandestine contact with King

Hussein, Rabin followed this strategy. His main concern, however, was to cement the strategic relationship with the USA, in which he succeeded both in terms of the funding as well as in terms of the new, modern equipment. This enabled Israel to re-establish both the reality, and the perception, of its deterrent power and relative strength.

The first Rabin administration came to an unhappy end in 1977 due to reasons which had little to do with his policies. Yet when looking at his consent, during his second term in 1993, to go ahead with the Oslo agreements, the basic analysis he gave me in 1976 had been vindicated:

- Israel was able to re-establish its military standing and its deterrence.
- Strategic relations with the US were established on the basis, both financial and substantive, envisaged by Rabin.
- The disappearance of the Soviet Union (unforeseen by Rabin, as by everyone else) also meant that the Arab countries lost their strategic ally.
- With the demise of Soviet power, the PLO was no longer a Soviet client, and the emergence of a PLO-headed state in the West Bank and Gaza would not create a Soviet foothold in the area.
- All these developments also had their impact on the PLO, which slowly (albeit reluctantly) moved from its military stance aimed at eliminating Israel to a less militant posture.

Many things changed between my long talk with Rabin in 1976 and the Oslo Accords in 1993. Rabin did not turn from a hawk into a dove; the circumstances he envisaged in 1976 fell into place, though it took longer than he imagined initially.

On a more theoretical level, Rabin expressed these views at a speech he delivered in October 1986 at a conference at Ben Gurion University in Be'er Sheva on the 1956 Suez-Sinai War. At that time he was Minister of Defence in the Shamir-Peres National Unity Government. Given the nature of the government and his subservient position in it – he was No. 3 – he chose to keep a low profile on issues of conflict resolution.

Yet the subject he chose for his lecture was significant. While many of the participants at the conference, who included British and French politicians, dwelt, some with visible nostalgia, on what they viewed as the lost opportunities of 1956, Rabin chose to speak on 'The Limits of Power', not the usual subject matter for ministers of defence.[1]

The crux of Rabin's lecture was his contention that Clausewitz's dictum, that war is merely the continuation of diplomacy by other means, cannot be sustained under

---

1. The following is based on the text of his lecture as published in: *The Suez-Sinai Crisis 1956: Retrospective and Reappraisal*, ed. by S I Troen & M Shemesh (London: Frank Cass, 1990), pp. 238-242.

contemporary conditions for a variety of general reasons, and specifically in the Arab-Israeli context.

According to Rabin, democracies, unless totally mobilised in a war against totalitarian dictatorships as in World War II, cannot follow the Clausewitzian dictum. In order to win a war in a democratic context, one has to be able to mobilise public opinion and manpower in ways which are different from the situation in Clausewitz's own time. Without being a neo-Kantian or a Wilsonian, Rabin realised the limits of power imposed by democratic values and institutions. 'Wars of Choice' cannot be easily waged by democracies. This was the cause of the Franco-British debacle at Suez, but he obviously also had the US in Vietnam in mind, though he did not say so. He explicitly dwelt on the 1982 'War of Choice' Israel waged in Lebanon and went into some detail explaining why Israel's strategy was doomed to fail. Forcing Lebanon to sign a peace treaty with Israel under conditions of occupation was a pipe dream: 'Through military means... the attempt to bring about a war that will end all wars is a dangerous course of action and an illusion'.

Rabin went on to argue that what the Allies were able to impose on Germany, Japan and Italy after 1945 cannot be achieved by Israel vis-à-vis the Arab countries. While he insisted that Israel needed a projection of its military power to deter Arab attempts to attack or try to destroy it, he concluded:

As I reflect on the long-term implications of this perception of the limits to our military power in the face of continuing threat from war and acts of terrorism, I have come to the conclusion that force of arms alone cannot bring about the desired termination of the Arab-Israeli conflict.

What Israel needs according to Rabin is 'commitment, patience and endurance', as there is no 'Dekhikat haKetz' [bringing about the end of days] nor does there exist a short-cut through 'zbeng v'gamarnu' [Hebrew slang for 'one shot, and it's over'].

I have chosen to dwell on these aspects of Rabin's thinking because, more than the usual encomiums, they seem to me to bring out the complexity of a man who always said he wanted to be a water engineer, but found himself involved in warfare – and peacemaking. They were the two sides of the same coin.

Shlomo Avineri is Professor of Political Science at the Hebrew University of Jerusalem and served as Director-General of Israel's Ministry of Foreign Affairs in the first government of Yitzhak Rabin.

The role of Britain
in Rabin's politics

by Rory Miller

Yitzhak Rabin was born in Jerusalem in March 1922. It was five years after the British Government issued the Balfour Declaration calling for the 'establishment in Palestine of a national home for the Jewish people', four years after General Edmund Allenby's army captured Palestine from the Ottoman Turks and three months prior to the League of Nations approval of a British mandate for Palestine, beginning a quarter century of formal British rule.

But the impact of Britain on Yitzhak Rabin precedes his birth. In his memoirs, Rabin notes that it was a British recruiting officer that was responsible for his surname as his father had changed it from Rubitzov while enrolling in the Jewish Legion during the First World War.

Rabin's childhood and teen years coincided with a period of great progress in the development of the Yishuv (the Jewish community in British mandate Palestine). These years saw the creation of extensive educational and welfare services, the building of landmark institutions, such as the Hebrew University of Jerusalem and the

Histadrut (the General Federation of Jewish Labour), which played a central role in building up the society and economy in a period of rising Jewish immigration.

Nor should we forget that the formative military experience of one of Israel's greatest soldiers began as a member of a unit of the Palmach (the elite section of the Yishuv's underground army) that cooperated with the British army in fighting axis forces in Syria and Lebanon between 1941 and 1943.

Yet despite all this, throughout his career the highly private Rabin remained ambivalent about the British role in mandatory Palestine and his own early life. For example, eschewing emotion, in his memoirs all he says about the relationship between the British mandatory authorities and the Yishuv was that it was 'schizophrenic at best' adding that in the two decades following the Balfour Declaration, 'the British had definitely reversed their policy of fostering a homeland for the Jews'.

Similarly, from his time as Chief of Staff of the Israel Defence Forces (IDF) between 1964 and 1967, which followed a period of study at Camberley Staff College in England, Rabin made the development of US-Israeli relations his number one international priority. Hence his request to be made Israel's ambassador to Washington following his retirement from the IDF in the wake of the June 1967 (Six Day) War. While, as Yoram Perri has written, during his time as the first Israeli-born Prime Minister between 1974 and 1977, 'more than any other Israeli politician, Rabin gave expression to his affinity to things American'.

Thus, unlike Golda Meir, his immediate predecessor as Prime Minister in the 1970s, Rabin did not form a close personal relationship, based on common socialist sympathies, with British Labour Prime Ministers Callaghan and Wilson. Unlike Menachem Begin, who made much of his admiration for Winston Churchill, Rabin refrained from public displays of admiration for Britain's great war-time leader.

Despite this, Rabin never forgot the centrality of Britain's role in establishing the Jewish National Home, and its deep influence on the development of the Yishuv and Israeli society post-1948. In a 1995 speech made only months prior to his murder, Rabin chose to recall:

> The happier moments between us: the Balfour Declaration, which established a national homeland for the Jewish people in Eretz Yisrael (the land of Israel), Britain's courageous stand during World War II in fighting the Nazi air blitz and all that we have absorbed of the British culture during the British Mandate. These will forever bind us together.

Moreover, though Rabin the soldier, diplomat and politician was one of the main architects and consolidators of Israeli-US relations over four decades, and though he publicly down-played the European (including the British) role in the region – on one occasion telling the German magazine, *Der Speigel* that 'the less Europeans meddle with the Middle East the better the chances for peace' – he was also well aware of the strategic, economic and political importance of Britain to Israel.

Rabin became Prime Minister for the first time in 1974, when Britain, though a shadow of its former imperial self, was still a leading western military power, a permanent member of the UN Security Council, not to mention a former colonial ruler of much of the Middle East, including Palestine. Like many of his political peers in Israel – most notably his foreign minister, Yigal Allon – he was very aware of the opportunity that Britain's 1973 entry into the European Economic Community provided Israel.

Firstly, Britain was a potential counter-balance to France, which since the late 1960s had been increasingly successful in steering the Community towards a pro-Arab Middle East policy. And though Britain joined its EEC partners in not allowing the US to use its territory to refuel supply planes destined for Israel during the 1973 Yom Kippur War, Rabin appreciated the fact that Britain, in the words of then Israeli ambassador Gideon Rafael, 'frustrated not only the attempts of the PLO in Britain, but [blocked] its efforts to attain recognition in the other EEC countries'.

Indeed, in a period when the PLO's twin policy of international terror and diplomacy was making major gains for the organisation in Europe, it was Britain's Labour leaders Wilson and Callaghan who most forthrightly opposed the normalisation of ties between the EEC and the PLO until the latter group renounced its goal of destroying the Jewish state. As Callaghan told the British parliament in 1977, 'I have made clear our position on the PLO. While it fails to recognise the existence of Israel and to deny that existence, I do not see how we can have dealings with it'.

Moreover, at the time of its entry into the EEC, Britain was Israel's third largest trading partner and an important market for Israeli agricultural produce (though overall Israel imported three times as much from the UK as it exported to her). Thus, by the time Rabin became premier in 1974, and primarily due to Britain's entry into the Community, trade with the EEC accounted for half of Israel's imports (c. US$2 billion) and a third of Israel's exports (c. US$700 million). The significance of this for the long-term development of the Israeli economy was not lost on Rabin, and led him to assure the Knesset in his first speech as Prime Minister that 'increased co-operation between us and... the Common Market in particular will now be one of the central objectives of the new government'.

In 1977, Rabin's Labor government was defeated in the general election by Likud and Menachem Begin replaced him as Prime Minister. From this time until its historic 1992 election victory under Rabin, Labor's only taste of government was in a National Unity coalition with the Likud between 1984 and 1990, during which time Rabin held the defence portfolio.

Though, as noted above, Begin had great admiration for Churchill, his antipathy towards Britain's role in Palestine during the mandate was barely concealed. This was reciprocated by much of the British political and media elite, who never forgave him for his role in attacks on British targets in Palestine, including the 1946 bombing of the British military headquarters at the King David hotel in Jerusalem. The same was true of Begin's Likud successor Yitzhak Shamir, whose own anti-British record during the 1940s was viewed as an irritant to Anglo-Israeli relations.

This explains, to some extent, the warm British reception that greeted Rabin's 1992 election victory. More importantly, if elected, Rabin had promised to make the promotion of peace with the Palestinians his government's 'central goal'. The British government shared the widespread optimism across the international arena that Rabin's accession to the premiership and the Labor victory had 'paved the way' for peace. Following Rabin's decision to embrace the Oslo peace process, ties between Israel and Britain reached an all-time high. Indeed, by the time John Major visited Israel in 1995, on the first British Prime Ministerial visit to Israel since Margaret Thatcher in 1986, the usually reticent Rabin was almost ebullient in his view that: 'We are witnessing today, close and very friendly relations between Jerusalem and London… We want you to know, Mr Prime Minister, that we see you and your people as dedicated partners and sincere friends. The Government and the State of Israel warmly shakes your hand and thanks you in appreciation'.

Just eight months later, and less than a week after the signing of the Oslo II agreement, Rabin was dead. His death sent shock waves across the world and, in Britain, the response was immediate and on a level not seen since the death of President John F Kennedy over thirty years earlier.

This expression of grief was not simply evidence of widespread British sympathy for Israel, or the Rabin family on their loss, but also underlined the concern that the death of such a key architect of the Oslo agreement might impact negatively on a permanent settlement between Israel and the Palestinians. In a memorial event held shortly after Rabin's death, then British foreign secretary Malcolm Rifkind, expressed this concern and borrowed from Victor Hugo to sum up Rabin's contribution to a comprehensive Arab-Israeli peace. 'Greater than the tread of mighty armies is an idea whose time has come', he told the massive crowd that flooded the auditorium and the streets surrounding the Royal Albert Hall to pay their respects to the slain Israeli leader.

On this tenth anniversary of Rabin's death, with Ariel Sharon's courageous removal of Jewish settlements from Gaza providing a glimmer of hope following a decade of misery and suffering, we could do worse than remember Hugo's words. But those who wish to contribute to Rabin's memory in a more practical way should also remember another major consideration for Rabin in pursuing peace with the Palestinians. He was driven in particular by his belief that, over the coming decades, Israel's security would face a far greater threat than that posed by the Palestinian problem if states like Iran succeeded in gaining a nuclear capability that could target the Jewish state.

Now many fear that this 'extremely grave development' —as Rabin termed it in a speech to the Knesset in July 1992 — is drawing near. Britain, in the company of Germany and France, has been working hard to find a compromise with Tehran that would prevent it gaining a nuclear weapons capability. It is only fitting that Britain use the tenth anniversary of Rabin's death, to confront a danger that had so preoccupied him in the final years of his life.

Dr Rory Miller is Senior Lecturer in Mediterranean and Middle East studies at King's College London.

Preserving democracy in the Jewish state: Rabin's driving imperatives

by Dennis Ross

It is hard to imagine that Yitzhak Rabin was assassinated ten years ago. At the time, I found it difficult to believe that Rabin, the Prime Minister and a man who had devoted his life to Israel and its security could be murdered by an Israeli. Here was a man whose life mirrored the state and its development. He fought for the creation of Israel as a young man and, as the Chief of Staff of the Israel Defence Forces, was the architect of its greatest military victory in June 1967.

He was a soldier but also a statesman. He was a superb analyst of the region and a leader with insight and courage. He was never complacent thinking about Israel's possibilities and problems. For him, Israel must retain its values and its character. He understood demographic trends and that is why he favoured partition.

Rabin understood that if Israel was to remain Jewish and democratic, it could not maintain its presence in the West Bank and Gaza. That would produce, in time, a reality where Jews were a minority in the area between the

Mediterranean Sea and the Jordan River and Israel could not be a place where a minority ruled a majority.

That is why Rabin understood that dividing the land with the Palestinians would be necessary. He hoped to do so through negotiations, in which case a genuine peace between two national movements might be achieved. Note how he spoke at the White House ceremony on September 13, 1993 of ending 'a hundred years of war'. He went in with his eyes open, not wishing away the past but also not willing to be paralysed by it.

He had no illusions. But he was guided by Israel's needs and was not prepared to sacrifice Israel's well-being and its security – practically and demographically – on the altar of an ideology that ignored the Palestinian presence in the West Bank and Gaza and the reality of their birth rates. Partition for Rabin would come either through negotiations or through unilateral separation behind a security fence or barrier.

For those who believe that Oslo was a mistake, Rabin, the realist, would remind them that standing pat was not an option. Palestinians would not have simply accepted continued Israeli occupation and domination. If Oslo did not pan out, if Palestinians would not fulfil their side of the bargain – a bargain that was security for Israelis, freedom for Palestinians – then Israel would separate from the Palestinians.

Prime Minister Sharon is not the father of the separation idea. Yitzhak Rabin was. Yitzhak Rabin, the realist, the soldier, the statesman, the patriot, saw it as a potential alternative. He wanted peace and believed it was possible. But he raised the idea of a security fence and separation from the Palestinians in 1995. If you want to know Yitzhak Rabin's legacy, it is not measured only in terms of his accomplishments for the State of Israel domestically and internationally. It is also measured in his profound belief in Israel's responsibility to retain its values and its belief in democracy – and to ensure its Jewish and democratic character. This will be his enduring legacy.

Ambassador Dennis Ross is counsellor and Ziegler distinguished fellow at The Washington Institute for Near East Policy. He was Special Middle East Coordinator under President Clinton and Director of the State Department's Policy Planning office under President George W H Bush.

The assassination of Rabin: attempting to nullify Oslo

by Colin Shindler

The murder of Yitzhak Rabin in November 1995 was a watershed in the Israeli far Right campaign of incitement against the Oslo Agreement. Yigal Amir, Rabin's assassin, was not considered insane or unbalanced before the killing, merely another right wing activist supporting the settlers. Yet it is clear that Amir was swept along by the rising tide of hatred. The language of the anti-Oslo campaign had moved from harsh criticism to chants of 'death to Rabin' amidst a sprinkling of rabbinical rulings, threats and curses.

An analysis three months before the killing had indicated that a tiny minority, 0.7%, endorsed the claim that 'a political assassination would be a correct deed if it would halt the peace process'. Rabin's personal survey researcher told him that there were at least 100 people who had the potential to carry out the act of murder.

The mainstream Right did not distance themselves from the rising paranoia. Likud leaders attended anti-Oslo demonstrations and referred to Rabin's Labor administration as 'a sick government'. Meanwhile, Benny Elon, until recently Minister for Tourism and a member of Moledet, a party which advocated 'transfer', warned that Rabin was precipitating civil war and that 'if he is not careful, he is liable to be killed'.

Labor responded by attacking its central parliamentary opponent, the Likud, rather than clamping down on the far Right and the radical settlers. Uzi Landau, ironically Sharon's main opponent against the recent Gaza disengagement in the Likud, responded by informing the daily Yediot Aharanot that Labor was spreading 'a blood libel against the Likud'.

Whatever Yigal Amir's motivation, the assassination of Yitzhak Rabin silenced the inciters and their targets into disbelief. The Jews had always regarded themselves as history's victims – the downtrodden and the powerless – they simply could not inflict violence on themselves in this fashion. Yigal Amir had shattered this self-delusion in the name of halting the historic reconciliation between Israelis and Palestinians.

On one level, the years after the historic handshake between Rabin and Arafat had been good ones for Israel. There had been economic prosperity, cooperation between Israelis and Palestinians in the peace process and the establishment of diplomatic relations with a large number of Arab states. However, the Oslo Agreement had created a large body of opposition within both Israel and the PLO. The Israeli Knesset had only endorsed it by 61 to 50. Likud leader Binyamin Netanyahu had called Oslo 'treason' while Moledet's Rehavam Ze'evi appealed to the military to defy the government. In the PLO Executive Committee of 18, five resigned and only nine were in favour.

Although a coalition of ten Palestinian groups, including rejectionists such as the Popular Front for the Liberation of Palestine, opposed Arafat, it was the advent of the Islamists that proved to be a decisive factor. Hamas had been formed shortly after the outbreak of the first Intifada in the late 1980s, but the running had been made by the smaller, more radical, Islamic Jihad. The latter was established shortly after the Islamic Revolution in Iran and followed in the footsteps of Ayatollah Khomeini. This, in itself, was remarkable, since the Palestinians were Sunni Muslims while the Iranians were Shi'ites.

Hamas, the political face of the Muslim Brotherhood in the West Bank and Gaza, rejected any contact with Iran for years for purely theological reasons. The end of the Iran-Iraq war and the Oslo Agreement pushed both sides together. Within a month of the White House handshake, Hamas embarked on a campaign of attacks on settlers, soldiers and civilians. Hamas imported from Iran the doctrine of self-sacrifice and suicide bombing, which originated during the Iran-Iraq war and was refined by Hezbollah's campaign against the Americans in Lebanon in the 1980s.

During Rabin's premiership, Hamas began its bombing campaign to wreck the peace process. While Oslo was certainly the cause, the indiscriminate killing of 30 Muslim worshippers in a Hebron mosque in 1994 by a radical settler, Baruch Goldstein, provided the retaliatory motivation. With settler rejectionists feeding Islamic rejectionists, the first bus bombings took place in Tel Aviv and Beit Lid.

Rabin's title of 'Mr Security' looked hollow and the enemies of Oslo made political capital. The opinion polls showed a sudden, but dramatic, drop in Rabin's support in favour of Netanyahu and the Likud. While Rabin's standing in the polls gradually recovered, the next bombing ensured that they once more plummeted. With each atrocity, the rate of recovery was slower. This followed the familiar pattern of the Israeli electorate's reaction to an outbreak of violence. It always catalysed a cosmic move to the Right. This happened when the first Intifada boosted the Likud in the election of 1988, enabling it to achieve victory.

Following Rabin's killing, the new Prime Minister Shimon Peres was 30 percentage points ahead in the polls. In all likelihood, many floating voters were revolted by the radicalism of the far right, and by association the Likud. But Hamas's actions at the beginning of 1996 – the first systematic campaign of suicide bombing in Israel's cities – unnerved and angered many. Moreover, it persuaded the floating voters to move back to the Likud. The bombers killed 87 Israeli civilians and injured over 200 in successive days in the heart of the country. The reaction of the Israeli electorate a few months later was to give Netanyahu a sliver of a majority and to place the opponents of Oslo in power.

The strength of Oslo was that it was based on a constructive ambiguity where Rabin and Arafat could 'do business' and make progress. The relationship between Arafat and Netanyahu, however, was one of polar opposites. Constructive ambiguity became specific certainty with

Netanyahu consistently pointing out Palestinian violations of agreements. Arafat, in turn, retaliated by listing Israeli violations. The failings of Arafat plus the increasing strength of the Islamists were further ingredients added into this witch's brew. If Oslo had provided a win-win scenario, the situation after Rabin's death meant a return to the 'them and us' syndrome. If Oslo symbolised a coming together of the Israeli and Palestinian peace camps against the rejectionists, the post-Rabin state of affairs resurrected the megaphone war and a return to 'Israel versus Palestine'.

Suppose fate had not taken its course on 4 November, 1995 and Rabin had stood in the 1996 election against Netanyahu. Would he have won? Would the reaction to the series of suicide bombings have swept Rabin away as it did Peres? Would Rabin's prestige have nullified the desire for security? All answers now reside within the realm of speculation. Probably Rabin would have done better than Peres, but the opinion polls showed Rabin trailing Netanyahu before his death.

If Netanyahu's tenure, 1996-1999, had been averted, there is every likelihood that the peace process would have fared better under a second term Rabin administration. The Rabin-Peres team would have provided the stability and rationality in policies that were subsequently missing. Perhaps there would have been an earlier evacuation of the Gaza settlements – and possibly of West Bank ones as well. The joker in the pack amidst such speculation is the global rise of Islamism. Could Rabin have succeeded in persuading Arafat to take action against religious extremists where others had failed? Probably not, but history under Rabin's responsible stewardship may still have taken a less bloody path.

Dr Colin Shindler is lecturer in Israeli and Modern Jewish Studies at the School of Oriental and African Studies, University of London.

Part III

Continuing the process: the legacy of Rabin

Israel's disengagement plan: carrying Rabin's torch

by Isaac Herzog MK

In the summer of 2005, Israel took the biggest step towards establishing a lasting peace between Israel and the Palestinians for 30 years, by withdrawing 8,000 of its citizens from the entire Gaza Strip and more than 300 sq miles of the northern West Bank. Disengagement from Gaza has ended the occupation of an estimated 1.4 million Palestinians. Gaza's Palestinian residents need no longer be disturbed by Israeli checkpoints and roadblocks and the evacuated settlements will help ease Gaza's crowding. Israel has shown that it is fully committed to a two-state solution and the path of peace which is Yitzhak Rabin's great legacy.

Israel made this happen through its determination to achieve peaceful coexistence, despite the obstacles placed in our way. It is important that observers around the world recognise the enormity of this step. Ariel Sharon's decision to withdraw from Gaza reversed a settlement policy he had supported for many years, dividing his supporters in the Knesset and alienating many of his party members.

He has endured death threats from Palestinian and Jewish extremists.

Many in Israel have noted, with great distress, parallels between the rhetoric used towards Sharon and other Israeli Government figures in response to the disengagement plan and the threats made towards Rabin in the period leading up to his death. Both Prime Ministers were called traitors and both have been compared to Nazis. Historic steps for peace take great courage.

It is heartening therefore, that this painful and difficult step for Israel has received such steadfast support from the British government and from around the world. The UK led the international community in recognising the significance of disengagement. Britain understands the importance of international encouragement and support to ensure that the peace process maintains momentum. The support Israel receives from the international community when taking steps for peace does not go unnoticed. It strengthens the arm of those of us who argue that bold steps for peace are of great benefit to the State of Israel.

However, those voices around the world that condemn Israel, whatever actions we take, make it harder for Israelis to make peace. When Israelis read the generalised attacks on Israel in some foreign papers, it feels as if we are being blamed for everything, including the terrorism that we suffer. Yet it is our children and families that are being killed and many of us feel great sympathy for Palestinian friends suffering just as much.

It is the terrorists who fire rockets from Gaza and send suicide bombers to Israeli shopping malls who undermine the peaceful hopes of moderate Palestinians and Israelis alike. Radicalised by ideologies of hate, they wish to see the end of the State of Israel and the creation of a fundamentalist Greater Palestine. Sadly, they have unwitting allies across the globe in the shape of those who support the isolation and demonisation of Israel.

Those who blame Israel for all the Middle East's problems, or claim that support for Israel is the reason for terror attacks elsewhere, are parroting the logic of the extremists. They are rewarding the terrorists who wish to destroy the region's only free and democratic country. From the very outset it has been terrorism which has caused setbacks in the peace process, not the other way around.

The desire to build a consensus for peace is nowhere stronger than among Israelis. Too many generations have grown up in fear of violence. That is why Yitzhak Rabin and Shimon Peres took great risks to pursue a new relationship with the Palestinians, despite many misgivings. Israelis have never had a guarantee that compromising on territory would bring an end to Palestinian violence. It is the goal of the terrorists to blow up those hopes of peace. So whilst Israel is ready to make compromises, major responsibility also lies with the Palestinian leadership and people to take real steps to improve security.

Palestinian violence undermines public confidence in a negotiated settlement. This is a political reality in Israel that is not well-understood outside it. The rejection of Ehud Barak's proposals at Camp David in 2000 and the conflict that followed made many Israelis sceptical that offers of peace would ever be seized by the Palestinian leadership. Those who make the case for peace are used to being met with the argument that such offers only get taken as a sign of weakness.

But despite these fears, the consensus in Israel remains in favour of a two-state solution. The process started by Rabin made it possible for the idea of a Palestinian state alongside Israel – once the preserve of the optimistic left – to become widely accepted across the political spectrum. The implementation of the disengagement plan reflects this understanding and has been the most tangible step yet towards making that vision a reality. We must reject any call for a one-state solution.

Disengagement from Gaza and part of the West Bank has firmly established the principle that peace will come by sharing the land and establishing borders. Removing sources of friction between the Israeli Defence Forces and ordinary Palestinians, even through a unilateral process, will make a negotiated settlement easier to achieve in the future. If tangible stability and development can be achieved in Gaza, support for violence will inevitably wither.

Neither the Oslo accords, nor the disengagement plan, came without pain and controversy. Indeed, the strain on our democratic values has been considerable, with large parts of Israeli society refusing to accept the Government's bold moves. But I firmly believe that we in Israel will move beyond our present disagreements. I believe that those who have opposed withdrawal from Gaza will eventually come to see why leaving Gaza was inevitable.

Just as the agreements that Rabin entered into marked a major turning point in the relationship between Israelis and Palestinians, so too the Gaza disengagement will be remembered as a vital step. If the Palestinians can control their own opposition forces and make democracy prevail, hope will be restored for Israelis and Palestinians alike. The responsibility for the international community is to reject the logic of the extremists, guard against demonisation of Israel and embrace all those taking steps towards peaceful coexistence and a two-state solution. Ten years after Rabin was assassinated, we must carry his torch.

Isaac Herzog is a Labor Knesset Member and the Minister of Construction and Housing in the Israeli government.

Can peace follow disengagement?

by Yossi Mekelberg

For many years the military and political careers of the late Israeli Prime Minister Yitzhak Rabin and current Prime Minister Ariel Sharon had crossed paths. During the Six Day War, when Rabin was the IDF Chief of Staff, Sharon was one of his youngest generals, and in later years they sought each other's advice and opinion, formally or informally, in whatever ministerial positions they held. Even at times of bitter political rivalry they remained not just close personal friends but also enjoyed mutual respect. This raises the question of how the slain Prime Minister would have assessed the policy towards resolving the Arab-Israeli conflict as carried out by the Israeli government ten years after his death.

The Oslo Accords might not initially have been the direction that Rabin wanted to pursue when he was returned to government in 1992, but it became the centrepiece of his government's policy till he met his death. Resolving the decades-long conflict with the Palestinians seemed for Rabin secondary to peace with Syria, which would have removed a major potential strategic threat to the existence of the Jewish state.

However, when he was presented by his Foreign Minister, Shimon Peres, with the opportunity for an historic breakthrough with the Palestinians, he gave it his full backing. Though warily, and some might say reluctantly, he signed the Oslo Accords which aimed to bring about an end to the conflict.

By nature, the Oslo process was gradual and cautious. But it implied in no uncertain terms that by the end of the process a Palestinian state would be established living in peace with Israel. This meant resolving the fundamental issues between the two nations including territorial disputes, the security of both independent states, an adequate solution to the Palestinian refugee problem and the future of Jerusalem as the capital of both Israel and Palestine.

Prime Minster Sharon's reading and attitude to the conflict is a departure from the Oslo process and Rabin's legacy regarding his approach to a settlement with the Palestinians. This is demonstrated by the disengagement plan from the Gaza Strip and by the building of a security barrier in the West Bank.

The underlying operative assumption that has driven Sharon's policy towards the conflict is that the Palestinians lack a leadership which is both willing and capable of reaching a genuine peace agreement with Israel, despite the death of Arafat and the election of Mahmoud Abbas as his moderate successor. The corollary has been that the foundation of the policy guaranteeing Israel's security and long-term well-being of its citizens has been unilateral in nature.

While the Oslo accords and its subsequent agreements were rooted in the recognition of the importance of mutuality in foreign affairs, the disengagement plan from Gaza and a small part of the West Bank is entrenched in the belief that Israel can enhance its security and separate from the Palestinians through a series of unilateral actions, as exemplified by the decision to build a security barrier between Israel and the Palestinians in the West Bank and to disengage from Gaza. The disengagement plan was conceived as a one-sided policy which needed no negotiation with the Palestinian Authority and no international involvement.

Furthermore, unlike the 1990s peace process which had a strategic horizon aimed at bringing finality to the conflict, the current goals of the Sharon government are more limited. The security barrier is aimed at protecting Israelis from the infiltration of Palestinians militants. The disengagement from Gaza aims to reduce the burden of defending isolated settlements and to consolidate Israel's position as a democratic state with a Jewish majority within recognised borders. Though comments from some in Sharon's administration have fuelled fears that the primary agenda is to strengthen Israel's hold on parts of the West Bank where nearly 80 percent of settlers live.

The plan can be seen to a certain degree, as Sharon himself has mentioned, as a reaction to a series of peace initiatives outside the political system, such as the Geneva Accords and the People's Voice, as well as the growing numbers of Israeli soldiers who refuse to serve in the occupied territories. Improving Israel's standing in the world – finally being seen as proactive in advancing the cause of peace in the region – was a bonus for Sharon.

The possibilities for the future are very open. If the situation now stagnates, it may mean a return to violence, but the precedent set by disengagement also shows that a final status solution may be possible through the Roadmap for peace. The implementation of the withdrawal gives important indications for the future, some of which are more positive than others.

Though the success of Sharon's unilateral approach has brought benefits, it has not been without unwanted costs for himself and Israel as a whole. More than the actual evacuation itself, which was conducted efficiently, sensitively and with much determination, it has been the political process which led to the disengagement that has left the Israeli political system, and to an extent Israeli society itself, exhausted and divided.

More than a year and a half of political wrangling saw the Prime Minister ignore a Likud party referendum when 60 percent of the participants opposed his plan. Two cabinet ministers were fired from the government to ensure a majority and two others resigned, in addition to, only a few days before the plan was implemented, Sharon's main political rival within the Likud Party, finance minister Binyamin Netanyahu.

Alongside to the problems around the decision making process, the 'orange' protest campaign led by those who opposed the disengagement plan was divisive and highly emotive. Comparisons between the Israeli government's actions and those taken by Nazi Germany in evacuating

Jews were not uncommon. Protestors also engaged in road blockades and the slashing of military vehicles' tyres.

For nearly a year and a half, the national agenda concentrated on a policy which was by nature limited. For some this casts doubt on the ability of Israel's political system and society to carry out the steps required for a comprehensive peace with the Palestinians.

Others fear that following disengagement, unilateral policies will provide the dominant paradigm for future Israeli policy towards the conflict. After all, few in the international community greeted the plan with much enthusiasm when it was first announced, but it ended with broad support, including the active participation of Egypt in securing the Philadelphi Route. The success of the security barrier in reducing Palestinian attacks further feeds the belief that unilateral action rather than bilateral or multilateral diplomacy is a better tool to advance Israel's national interest.

Overall, the decision making process in Israel was exposed as volatile, lacking strategic vision and ad hoc by nature. A policy which enjoyed from its outset a solid support of around 70% of the population faced persistent and stubborn resistance which caused unnecessary delay in its implementation. Opposition came both from within the political party system and from a vociferous, dynamic and well organised campaign by the settler lobby.

But despite these fears, the precedent set in the summer of 2005 also gives considerable cause for optimism. All the inhabitants were evacuated from their settlements within six days without any bloodshed, despite some dire predictions. All resistance was easily overcome by the Israeli army and police. The efficiency with which more than 15,000 people were removed from the 21 settlements dispels the myth of the irreversibility of the settlement project, even in the West Bank.

Another precedent set is the involvement of Egypt in the political process between Israel and the Palestinians. President Hosni Mubarak played a significant role in mediating between the Palestinian Authority and Hamas and other religious fundamentalist groups to ensure that the latter would not try and sabotage the disengagement by attacking Israel. The entire operation passed with minimal attacks on Israeli targets, which is a positive sign for future peace negotiations.

Having considered the precedents, both positive and negative, set by the disengagement plan, the question remains how to move forward from here. As successful as the disengagement was, it was still at best a first step towards a comprehensive peace agreement. For peace to become a reality, Israelis and Palestinians must return to the negotiating table and to the Roadmap.

Some have seen the plan as a complete departure from the Roadmap, but for others it was only a temporary diversion. The Palestinian elected leadership, with help from the outside, now has the opportunity to assert its authority by making the Gaza Strip an economic success and by building democratic and accountable institutions. It must also reassure Israel's citizens that giving up land does not encourage militancy, through the active prevention of rocket and suicide bomber attacks.

Israel also needs to keep momentum by improving life for Palestinians in the West Bank. Freedom of movement is limited due to the many scattered checkpoints and the route of the security barrier. Both need to be rethought to reflect the new opportunity to advance peace. Furthermore, the Israeli Government is obliged to fulfil its commitment to remove all illegal outposts in the West Bank and can improve the political atmosphere by reducing settlement activity elsewhere.

For its part, the international community, especially the United States and the European Union, also needs to be proactive in promoting a solution based on two states living side by side in peace. This can be done through active mediation, ensuring that both sides fulfil their international obligations, and setting a new timetable for reaching a final status agreement. Without such active involvement it is hard to see a comprehensive agreement, which addresses all the outstanding issues between the two nations, being reached.

Ten years after the cruel death of Prime Minister Rabin, bringing an end to the decades-long conflict between Israelis and Palestinians seems to be the ultimate way to honour his sacrifice for peace.

Professor Yossi Mekelberg is the Head of International Relations Department at Webster/BACL, Regent's College, London and an Associate Fellow of the Middle East Programme at Chatham House.

Part IV

Rabin in his own words

Lecture on receiving the Nobel Peace Prize December 10, 1994

by Yitzhak Rabin

Your Majesty the King,
Your Royal Highness,
Esteemed Members of the Norwegian Nobel Committee,
Honourable Prime Minister, Madame Gro Harlem Brundtland,
Ministers,
Members of the Parliament and Ambassadors,
Fellow laureates,
Distinguished guests,
Friends,
Ladies and gentlemen.

At an age when most youngsters are struggling to unravel the secrets of mathematics and the mysteries of the Bible; at an age when first love blooms; at the tender age of sixteen, I was handed a rifle so that I could defend myself – and also, unfortunately, so that I could kill in an hour of danger.

That was not my dream. I wanted to be a water engineer. I studied in an agricultural school and I thought that being a water engineer was an important profession in the parched Middle East. I still think so today. However, I was compelled to resort to the gun.

I served in the military for decades. Under my command, young men and women who wanted to live, wanted to love, went to their deaths instead. Under my command, they killed the enemy's men who had been sent out to kill us.

Ladies and gentlemen,

In my current position, I have ample opportunity to fly over the State of Israel, and lately over other parts of the Middle East, as well. The view from the plane is breathtaking: deep-blue lakes, dark-green fields, dun-coloured deserts, stone-grey mountains, and the entire countryside peppered with whitewashed, red-roofed houses.

And cemeteries. Graves as far as the eye can see.

Hundreds of cemeteries in our part of the Middle East – in our home in Israel – but also in Egypt, in Syria, Jordan, Lebanon, and Iraq. From the plane's window, from thousands of feet above them, the countless tombstones are silent. But the sound of their outcry has carried from the Middle East throughout the world for decades.

Standing here today, I wish to salute loved ones – and foes. I wish to salute all the fallen of all the countries in all the wars; the members of their families who bear the enduring burden of bereavement; the disabled whose scars will never heal. Tonight I wish to pay tribute to each and every one of them, for this important prize is theirs, and theirs alone.

Ladies and gentlemen,

I was a young man who has now grown fully in years. And of all the memories I have stored up in my seventy-two years, what I shall remember most, to my last day, are the silences.

The heavy silence of the moment after, and the terrifying silence of the moment before.

As a military man, as a commander, I issued orders for dozens, probably hundreds of military operations. And together with the joy of victory and grief of bereavement, I shall always remember the moment just after making the decision to mount an action: the hush as senior officers or cabinet ministers slowly rise from their seats; the sight of their receding backs; the sound of the closing door; and then the silence in which I remain alone.

That is the moment you grasp that as a result of the decision just made, people will be going to their deaths. People from my nation, people from other nations. And they still don't know it.

At that hour, they are still laughing and weeping; still weaving plans and dreaming about love; still musing about planting a garden or building a house – and they have no idea these are their last hours on earth. Which of them is fated to die? Whose picture will appear in a black border in tomorrow's newspaper? Whose mother will soon be in mourning? Whose world will crumble under the weight of the loss?

As a former military man, I will also forever remember the silence of the moment before: the hush when the hands of the clock seem to be spinning forward, when time is running out and in another hour, another minute, the inferno will erupt.

In that moment of great tension just before the finger pulls the trigger, just before the fuse begins to burn; in the terrible quiet of that moment, there's still time to wonder, alone: Is it really imperative to act? Is there no other choice? No other way?

And then the order is given, and the inferno begins.

'God takes pity on kindergarteners', wrote the poet Yehudah Amichai, who is here with us tonight,

'God takes pity on kindergarteners,
Less so on schoolchildren,
And will no longer pity their elders,
Leaving them to their own.
And sometimes they will have to crawl on all fours
Through the burning sand
To reach the casualty station
Bleeding.'

For decades God has not taken pity on the kindergarteners in the Middle East, or the schoolchildren, or their elders. There has been no pity in the Middle East for generations.

Ladies and gentlemen,

I was a young man who has now grown fully in years. And of all the memories I have stored up in my seventy-two years, I now recall the hopes.

Our peoples have chosen us to give them life. Terrible as it is to say, their lives are in our hands. Tonight, their eyes are upon us and their hearts are asking: How is the authority vested in these men and women being used? What will they decide? What kind of morning will we rise to tomorrow? A day of peace? Of war? Of laughter or of tears?

A child is born into an utterly undemocratic world. He cannot choose his father and mother. He cannot pick his sex or colour, his religion, nationality, or homeland. Whether he is born in a manor or a manger, whether he lives under a despotic or democratic regime, it is not his choice. From the moment he comes, close-fisted, into the world, his fate lies in the hands of his nation's leaders. It is they who will decide whether he lives in comfort or despair, in security or in fear. His fate is given to us to resolve – to the Presidents and Prime Ministers of countries, democratic or otherwise.

Ladies and gentlemen,

Just as no two fingerprints are identical, so no two people are alike, and every country has its own laws and culture, traditions and leaders. But there is one universal message which can embrace the entire world, one precept which can be common to different regimes, to races which bear no resemblance, to cultures alien to each other.

It is a message which the Jewish people has borne for thousands of years, a message found in the Book of Books, which my people has bequeathed to all civilized men: 'V'nishmartem me'od lnafshoteichem', in the words in Deuteronomy; 'Therefore take good heed to yourselves' – or, in contemporary terms, the message of the sanctity of life.

The leaders of nations must provide their peoples with the conditions – the 'infrastructure', if you will – which enables them to enjoy life: freedom of speech and of movement; food and shelter; and most important of all: life itself. A man cannot enjoy his rights if he is not among the living. And so every country must protect and preserve the key element in its national ethos: the lives of its citizens.

To defend those lives, we call upon our citizens to enlist in the army. And to defend the lives of our citizens serving in the army, we invest huge sums in planes, and tanks, in armoured plating and concrete fortifications. Yet despite it all, we fail to protect the lives of our citizens and soldiers. Military cemeteries in every corner of the world are silent testimony to the failure of national leaders to sanctify human life.

There is only one radical means of sanctifying human lives. Not armoured plating, or tanks, or planes, or concrete fortifications.

The one radical solution is peace.

Ladies and gentlemen,

The profession of soldiering embraces a certain paradox. We take the best and bravest of our young men into the army. We supply them with equipment which costs a virtual fortune. We rigorously train them for the day when they must do their duty – and we expect them to do it well. Yet we fervently pray that that day will never come – that the planes will never take flight, the tanks will never move forward, the soldiers will never mount the attacks for which they have been trained so well.

We pray it will never happen because of the sanctity of life.

History as a whole, and modern history in particular, has known harrowing times when national leaders turned their citizens into cannon fodder in the name of wicked doctrines: vicious Fascism and fiendish Nazism. Pictures of children marching to the slaughter, photos of terrified women at the gates of crematoria must loom before the eyes of every leader in our generation, and the generations to come. They must serve as a warning to all who wield power.

Almost all the regimes which did not place man and the sanctity of life at the heart of their world view, all those regimes have collapsed and are no more. You can see it for yourselves in our own day.

Yet this is not the whole picture. To preserve the sanctity of life, we must sometimes risk it. Sometimes there is no other way to defend our citizens than to fight for their lives, for their safety and sovereignty. This is the creed of every democratic state.

Ladies and gentlemen,

In the State of Israel, from which I come today; in the Israel Defence Forces, which I have had the privilege to command, we have always viewed the sanctity of life as a supreme value. We have gone to war only when a fearful sword was poised to cut us down.

The history of the State of Israel, the annals of the Israel Defence Forces are filled with thousands of stories of soldiers who sacrificed themselves – who died while trying to save wounded comrades; who gave their lives to avoid causing harm to innocent people on the enemy's side.

In the coming days, a special commission of the Israel Defence Forces will finish drafting a code of conduct for our soldiers. The formulation regarding human life will read as follows, and I quote:

'In recognition of its supreme importance, the soldier will preserve human life in every way possible and endanger himself, or others, only to the extent deemed necessary to fulfil this mission.

The sanctity of life, in the view of the soldiers of the Israel Defence Forces, will find expression in all their actions; in considered and precise planning; in intelligent and safety-minded training and in judicious implementation, in accordance with their mission; in taking the professionally proper degree of risk and degree of caution; and in the constant effort to limit casualties to the scope required to achieve the objective.' End quote.

For many years ahead – even if wars come to an end, after peace comes to our land – these words will remain a pillar of fire which goes before our camp, a guiding light for our people. And we take pride in that.

Ladies and gentlemen,

We are in the midst of building the peace. The architects and engineers of this enterprise are engaged in their work even as we gather here tonight, building the peace layer by layer, brick by brick, beam by beam. The job is difficult, complex, trying. Mistakes could topple the whole structure and bring disaster down upon us.

And so we are determined to do the job well – despite the toll of murderous terrorism, despite fanatic and scheming enemies.

We will pursue the course of peace with determination and fortitude.

We will not let up.

We will not give in.

Peace will triumph over all our enemies, because the alternative is grim for us all.

And we will prevail.

We will prevail because we regard the building of peace as a great blessing for us, and for our children after us. We regard it as a blessing for our neighbours on all sides, and for our partners in this enterprise – the United States, Russia, Norway, and all mankind.

We wake up every morning, now, as different people. Suddenly, peace. We see the hope in our children's eyes. We see the light in our soldiers' faces, in the streets, in the buses, in the fields.

We must not let them down.

We will not let them down.

I do not stand here alone, today, on this small rostrum in Oslo. I am the emissary of generations of Israelis, of the shepherds of Israel, just as King David was a shepherd, of the herdsmen and dressers of sycamore trees, as the prophet Amos was; of the rebels against the establishment, like the prophet Jeremiah, and of men who go down to the sea, like the prophet Jonah.

I am the emissary of the poets and of those who dreamed of an end to war, like the prophet Isaiah.

I am also the emissary of sons of the Jewish people like Albert Einstein and Baruch Spinoza; like Maimonides, Sigmund Freud, and Franz Kafka.

And I am the emissary of the millions who perished in the Holocaust, among whom were surely many Einsteins and Freuds who were lost to us, and to humanity, in the flames of the crematoria.

I am here as the emissary of Jerusalem, at whose gates I fought in days of siege; Jerusalem which has always been, and is today, the eternal capital of the State of Israel and the heart of the Jewish people, who pray toward it three times a day.

And I am also the emissary of the children who drew their visions of peace; and of the immigrants from St Petersburg and Addis Ababa.

I stand here mainly for the generations to come, so that we may all be deemed worthy of the medallion which you have bestowed on me today.

I stand here as the emissary of our neighbours who were our enemies. I stand here as the emissary of the soaring hopes of a people which has endured the worst that history has to offer and nevertheless made its mark – not just on the chronicles of the Jewish people but on all mankind.

With me here are five million citizens of Israel – Jews and Arabs, Druze and Circassians – five million hearts beating for peace – and five million pairs of eyes which look to us with such great expectations for peace.

Ladies and gentlemen,

I wish to thank, first and foremost, those citizens of the State of Israel, of all generations and political persuasions, whose sacrifices and relentless struggle for peace bring us steadier closer to our goal.

I wish to thank our partners – the Egyptians, Jordanians, Palestinians, and the Chairman of the Palestinian Liberation Organisation, Mr Yasser Arafat, with whom we share this Nobel Prize – who have chosen the path of peace and are writing a new page in the annals of the Middle East.

I wish to thank the members of the Israeli government and above all my colleague Mr Shimon Peres, whose energy and devotion to the cause of peace are an example to us all.

I wish to thank my family for their support.

And, of course, I wish to thank the members of the Nobel Committee and the courageous Norwegian people for bestowing this illustrious honour on my colleagues and myself.

Ladies and gentlemen,

Allow me to close by sharing with you a traditional Jewish blessing which has been recited by my people, in good times and in bad, from time immemorial, as a token of their deepest longing:

'The Lord will give strength to his people; the Lord will bless his people – all of us – with peace.'

Index